Writer's Handbook

Rigby
A Harcourt Achieve Imprint

www.Rigby.com
1-800-531-5015

Table of Contents

Introduction

Questions about writing pop up all the time, and we don't always have the answers. When do I capitalize the word **mother?** What's the correct abbreviation for **ounce?** If you don't know the answer, you really need to know where to find it.

The **Writer's Handbook** has all kinds of answers to questions about writing. It covers rules for spelling, capitalization, punctuation, and grammar. Think of the **Writer's Handbook** as a place to find answers.

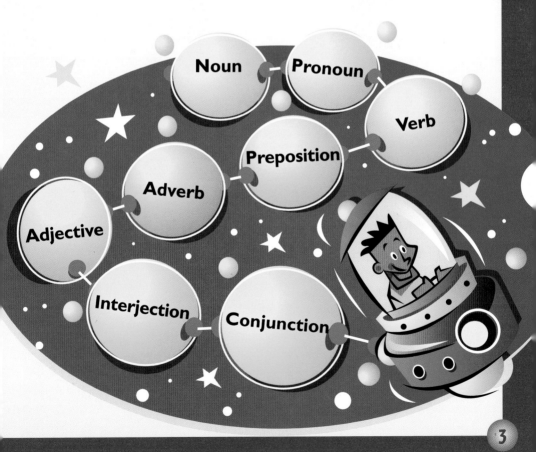

Capitalization

If you learn the basics of capitalization, you'll be more confident as a writer.

Proper Nouns/Proper Adjectives

Capitalize all proper nouns and proper adjectives. A **proper noun** is the name of a specific person, place, or thing. When a proper noun is used to describe something, it is called a proper adjective.

Proper Nouns Tiger Woods, New York Yankees

Proper Adjectives Chicago pizza, an English garden

> **Tip**
> The first letter of first, middle, and last names is always capitalized.

Names of People

Capitalize the first letter of first, middle, and last names. Capitalize the initials that stand for those names.

- Christopher Columbus
- Dr. Martin Luther King, Jr.
- J. K. Rowling

Titles Used with Names

Capitalize titles used with names of people.

- Queen Elizabeth
- President Kennedy
- Mayor Lopez

> **Tip**
> Do not capitalize titles when used without a name: *the queen, the president, the mayor.*

J.K. Rowling

Words Used as Names

Capitalize words that are used as names, such as *Mother*, *Father*, *Grandma*, and *Grandpa*.

- When I visit, <u>Grandpa</u> usually makes me lunch. (In this case, *Grandpa* is used as a first name.)
- My <u>grandpa</u> usually gives me a hug when I visit. (In this case, *grandpa* is not used as a first name.)

Organizations

Capitalize names of teams, organizations, businesses, and political groups.

- Arizona Cardinals
- Boy Scouts of America
- Democratic Party
- Republicans

Days, Months, and Holidays

Capitalize the names of the days of the week, months of the year, and holidays.

Days Monday, Friday

Months January, May

Holidays Easter, Passover

Religions, Nationalities, Languages

Capitalize names of religions, nationalities, and languages.

Religions Christian, Muslim

Nationalities Egyptian, Australian

Languages Spanish, Japanese

Tip

Capitalize the names of companies and the official names of products. Do not capitalize a general name for a product, such as *cereal* or *shampoo*.

Tiger Woods

Grandma

Chicago Pizza

Titles

Capitalize the first and last word of a title. Capitalize every word in between that is not an article (*a, an, the*), a short preposition (*in, of, on,* etc.), or short conjunction (*and, or,* etc.).

Book *The Lion, the Witch, and the Wardrobe*

Movie *The Wizard of Oz*

Historical Information

Capitalize the names of:

Historical events American Civil War

Documents Bill of Rights

Abbreviations

Capitalize abbreviations of titles and organizations.

M.D. (Doctor of Medicine)

NBA (National Basketball Association)

NFL (National Football League)

First Words

Capitalize the first word of a sentence.

- The movie earned 15 million dollars in its opening weekend.

Capitalize the first word of a direct quotation.

- One critic said, "The movie will be a great success."

Tip

Don't be fooled! Not all short words are articles, prepositions, or conjunctions. Be sure to capitalize short words such as *Red*, *End*, and *Not*.

Greetings and Closings of Letters

Capitalize the first letter in the greeting. Also capitalize the first letter in the closing.

Greeting Dear Jane,

Closing Your friend,
Mario

Names of Places and Things

Capitalize all of the following:

Planets Earth, Saturn

Continents Europe, Asia

Countries Japan, Norway

Sections of the Country the South, the Northeast

States California, Georgia

Provinces Ulster, Quebec

Cities and Counties New Orleans, Cook County

Bodies of Water Atlantic Ocean, Irish Sea, Mississippi River

Mountains Rocky Mountains, Andes, Alps

Public Areas Yellowstone National Park, Lincoln Memorial

Roads and Highways Frontage Road, 17th Avenue, Interstate 70

Buildings Empire State Building, John Hancock Building

TechTip

| CAPS LOCK key | When you are typing on a computer, use the CAPS LOCK key or press SHIFT and the letter key to capitalize a letter. |
| SHIFT + the letter key | |

Tip

Do not capitalize names of the seasons (*winter*, *spring*, *summer*, *fall*) or directions (*north*, *south*, *east*, *west*).

Punctuation

As you write, do you ever wonder where to place a comma or when to start a new sentence? You already know many of the rules of punctuation. After all, you punctuate your speech whenever you talk to someone. Read the examples below and see just how important correct punctuation can be.

Without punctuation:

- Keisha was worried about her test she had a basketball game that afternoon and the team was counting on her to play well Keisha would have to be rested calm and relaxed she would definitely have to be happy with her test score.

With punctuation:

- Keisha was worried about her test. She had a basketball game that afternoon, and the team was counting on her. To play well, Keisha would have to be rested, calm, and relaxed. She would definitely have to be happy with her test score.

You can easily learn the basics of punctuation. Read on to find out more!

Period .

Use a period to end a sentence and to mark abbreviations, initials, and decimal points.

At the End of a Sentence

- Joe's birthday party lasted well past dark.

After Abbreviations

- Dr., Mrs., Mr., Ph.D., etc., vs., ex., A.M., P.M.

Use only one period when an abbreviation marks the end of a sentence.

- Our teacher uses the title of Ms.

After Initials

- C. S. Lewis
- Booker T. Washington

As a Decimal

- Don's temperature was a feverish 101.1 degrees.
- Isabel was overcharged by $1.50 at the store.

eggs , juice , and bread

Comma ,

Commas help the reader know where to pause. Use a comma to break up words and ideas and to make sentences clear. Commas are essential in the following situations:

Items in a Series

Use a comma to separate words, phrases, or clauses in a series.

Words My mom picked up eggs, juice, and bread at the grocery store.

Phrases Sean enjoys playing basketball, hiking in the mountains, and riding horses.

In Dates and Addresses

Use a comma to separate items in dates and addresses.

Date The Declaration of Independence was signed on July 4, 1776.

Address Audrey's new address is 1200 Montview Street, Denver, Colorado 80207.

To Set Off Dialogue

Use a comma to separate the words of a speaker from the rest of the sentence.

- The boxer Muhammad Ali said, "I am the greatest."

Do not use a comma when you are merely reporting what someone said.

- Jake said that the test was easy.

In Direct Address

Use a comma to separate a noun of direct address (the person to whom one is speaking) from the rest of the sentence.

- Alonso, it's so nice to meet you!

In Letter Writing

Use a comma after the greeting and closing in friendly letters.

Greeting Dear Grandpa Leo,

Closing With love,

Tip

In business letters, use a *colon* (:) after the greeting.

Dear Sir:

To Separate Adjectives

Use a comma to separate two or more adjectives if:

you can switch the order of the adjectives and the sentence still reads clearly.

- I dislike cold, runny eggs.
- I dislike runny, cold eggs.

you can put *and* between the adjectives and still have the sentence read clearly.

- I dislike cold and runny eggs.

No commas are used when the order of the adjectives *cannot* be switched.

- I dislike cold scrambled eggs.

In Numbers

Use a comma in numbers of four digits or more to keep the numbers clear.

- Cathy's car was still running strong after 150,000 miles.

To Set Off Interruptions

Use a comma to set off a word, phrase, or clause that interrupts the main idea of a sentence.

- Cathy was, however, longing to drive a newer car.
- Cathy, my oldest sister, takes me to school every day.

Between Two Independent Clauses

Use a comma between two independent clauses that are joined by a coordinating conjunction.

- Ming doesn't like the color blue, so she bought the purple bike.
- I'm tired today, but I have no time for a nap.

To Set Off Interjections

Use a comma to separate an interjection or short exclamation from the rest of the sentence.

- Whoa, slow down!
- Hey, cut it out!

To Set Off Appositives

An appositive is a word or phrase that follows a noun or pronoun and explains more about it. It renames the noun or pronoun before it. Use a comma to set off the appositive.

- My aunt, a bowler, takes her bowling ball on vacation.

To Set Off Long Phrases and Clauses

Use a comma to set off a long modifying phrase or clause from a clause that follows it.

- After standing in the lunch line for so long, I was ready to eat everything on the menu.
- When Jorge moved to a different city, he worried about making new friends.

Semicolon ;

The semicolon works both as a comma and a period. It is used:

Between Independent Clauses

Use a semicolon to join two or more independent clauses that may each stand alone as a separate sentence.

- My older brother gets to stay up later than I do; I can't wait to be his age.

To Separate Phrases

Use a semicolon to separate a series of phrases that already have commas.

- People everywhere should drive less; recycle cans, glass, and paper; and save energy.

Colon :

A colon introduces a list or prepares the reader for information that follows. It is also used between numbers in time.

To Introduce a List

Use a colon to introduce a list.

- Dad wanted to buy a number of things at the store: milk, cheese, toothpaste, and soap.

To Introduce a Long or Important Quotation

Use a colon to introduce a long or important quotation.

- The Declaration of Independence states: "We hold these truths to be self-evident, that all men are created equal . . . ."

Between Numbers in Time

Use a colon to separate the minutes from the hour.

- School starts at 8:10 A.M.

Hyphen −

A hyphen may divide or join words. It can also be used to create new words.

To Divide a Word

Use a hyphen to divide a word when you run out of room at the end of a line. A word can be divided only between its syllables. One-syllable words can't be divided.

- Spring is my favorite season because many trees blossom at that time of year.

With a Certain Prefix

Use a hyphen with certain prefixes.

- ex-coach, mid-July, half-asleep, self-defense

Prefixes ex, mid, half, self

Use a hyphen to join two or more words before a noun to create an adjective.

- Teddy was an ill-mannered terrier.

Dash —

Use a dash to show a sudden break in the sentence or to show that a speaker has been interrupted.

In a Sentence Break

Use a dash to show a sudden break in a sentence, such as a change in thought or direction.

- My dad—in case you hadn't noticed—is very funny.

In Interrupted Speech

Use a dash to show that another person is interrupting someone's speech.

- Oh, hi—no, I hadn't heard— that's great news.

Ellipsis •••

Use an ellipsis to show that words or sentences have been omitted or to show a pause in dialogue.

To Show Omitted Words

Use an ellipsis to show that one or more words have been omitted from a quotation.

Tip

When you type an ellipsis in the middle of a sentence, leave a space before, after, and in between each of the three periods.

Complete quote "The only thing I can be sure of is that the play begins at 9 o'clock and that we'll lose our seats if we don't arrive on time."

Shortened quote " . . . the play begins at 9 o'clock . . . we'll lose our seats if we don't arrive on time."

Tip

If the ellipses are at the end of a sentence, use four periods and leave a space before, after, and in between each period.

Pause in Dialogue

Use an ellipsis to show a pause in dialogue, or at the end where dialogue trails off.

- "I'm . . . shocked!"
- "I was shocked . . . ."

Quotation Marks " "

Quotation marks go around the exact words of a speaker and around titles.

Direct Quotations

Use quotation marks before and after spoken words.

- Patrick Henry said, "Give me liberty or give me death!"

Placement of Punctuation

Place quotation marks around text that contains periods and commas.

- "Maria, don't forget to water the plants," said Mom.
- Maria replied, "I'll do it later, Mom."

A question mark or exclamation point is placed inside the quotation marks when it punctuates the sentence in the quotes.

- "Maria, do you want to get your allowance this week?" asked Mom.

It is placed outside the quotation marks when it punctuates the main sentence.

- Do you ever tell your parents, "I'll do it later"?

To Punctuate Titles

Use quotation marks to punctuate titles of songs, poems, stories, essays, magazine articles, and chapters of books.

Song "America the Beautiful"

Poem "Casey at the Bat"

Story "Second-Hand Man"

Essay "Mother Tongue"

Article "The Life of a Killer Whale"

Chapter of a Book "Miranda's Charm"

"I'll do it later, Mom."

To Punctuate Words for Emphasis

Use quotation marks around words in a sentence that you want to emphasize for a special reason or call out in order to make a point to the reader.

- She had a great "excuse" for not coming to the party.

Question Mark ?

A question mark shows curiosity.

Direct Question

Use a question mark at the end of a question.

- How old are you?

Exclamation Point !

An exclamation point expresses strong emotion. It is placed after a word, phrase, or sentence.

Word Oh!

Phrase Happy New Year!

Sentence I'm so excited about summer vacation!

Italics and Underlines

Italics and underlines are used to highlight titles and for emphasizing. Use italics when typing on a computer. Underline when you write by hand.

For Titles

Use italics or underlining for titles of plays, books, newspapers, magazines, movies, or CDs.

Play *Romeo and Juliet*, Romeo and Juliet

Book *Sounder*; Sounder

Movie *Peter Pan*, Peter Pan

For Specific Words

Use italics or underlining to show emphasis in a sentence.

- That is one *big* tree!
- That is one big tree!

Parentheses ( )

Parentheses are placed around certain words in a sentence to add information or to make an idea clearer.

To Add Information

Use parentheses to show information that should not stand out.

- The graph (figure 3) shows the rise in accidents on scooters.

Common Abbreviations

An abbreviation is the shortened form of a word or phrase. Most abbreviations begin with a capital letter and end with a period. Here are some common abbreviations:

- Mr., Mrs., Ms., Dr., M.D., B.C., A.D., A.M., P.M.

These are acceptable in all types of writing.

Tip

In formal writing, do not abbreviate the names of states, countries, months, days, or units of measure.

Other forms of abbreviations are:

Acronyms

An acronym is a word that is formed from the first letter or letters of words in a phrase. Acronyms do not use periods.

NASA (National Aeronautics and Space Administration)

RADAR (Radio Detection and Ranging)

SCUBA (Self-Contained Underwater Breathing Apparatus)

Initialisms

An initialism is different from an acronym. Initialisms are not pronounced as words but as separate letters.

POW (Prisoner of War)

FBI (Federal Bureau of Investigation)

TV (television)

State Abbreviations

Alabama	AL
Alaska	AK
Arizona	AZ
Arkansas	AR
California	CA
Colorado	CO
Connecticut	CT
Delaware	DE
District of Columbia	DC
Florida	FL
Georgia	GA
Hawaii	HI
Idaho	ID
Illinois	IL
Indiana	IN
Iowa	IA
Kansas	KS
Kentucky	KY
Louisiana	LA
Maine	ME
Maryland	MD
Massachusetts	MA
Michigan	MI
Minnesota	MN
Mississippi	MS
Missouri	MO
Montana	MT
Nebraska	NE
Nevada	NV

New Hampshire	NH
New Jersey	NJ
New Mexico	NM
New York	NY
North Carolina	NC
North Dakota	ND
Ohio	OH
Oklahoma	OK
Oregon	OR
Pennsylvania	PA
Rhode Island	RI
South Carolina	SC
South Dakota	SD
Tennessee	TN
Texas	TX
Utah	UT
Vermont	VT
Virginia	VA
Washington	WA
West Virginia	WV
Wisconsin	WI
Wyoming	WY

Address Abbreviations

Apartment	Apt.
Avenue	Ave.
Boulevard	Blvd.
Court	Ct.
Drive	Dr.
East	E.
Expressway	Expwy.
Heights	Hts.
Highway	Hwy.
Lane	Ln.
North	N.
Park	Pk.
Parkway	Pkwy.
Place	Pl.
Road	Rd.
Rural	R.
South	S.

Square	Sq.
Station	Sta.
Street	St.
Terrace	Ter.
Turnpike	Tnpk.
West	W.

Weights and Measures

teaspoon	tsp
tablespoon	T
ounce	oz
cup	c
pint	pt
milliliter	ml
liter	L
quart	qt
gallon	gal
millimeter	mm
centimeter	cm
meter	m
inch	in.
foot	ft
yard	yd
milligram	mg
gram	g
kilogram	kg
pound	lb
mile	mi
kilometer	km
Celsius	C
Fahrenheit	F

Contractions and Apostrophes

Many people use contractions such as *I'm* instead of *I am*, or *don't* instead of *do not*. A contraction is the shortened form of two words. An apostrophe shows where one or more letters are missing. It is quite common to use contractions in both writing and speaking. Before learning about contractions, you need to know about apostrophes.

Apostrophes

An apostrophe forms plurals, shows that one or more letters have been omitted from a word, or shows possession.

To Form Plurals

Do not use an apostrophe to create the plural of a letter or number.

Letter Bs
Number 3s
Year 1930s

In Contractions

Use an apostrophe to show that one or more letters are missing.

- she'd = she would, she had
- I'm = I am
- you're = you are
- don't = do not
- they'll = they will
- o'clock = of the clock

In Singular Possessives

Use an apostrophe and *s* to form the singular possessive.

- My <u>cousin's</u> skateboard is missing a wheel.

When the possessive has one syllable and ends in an *s* or *z* sound, add an apostrophe and *s*.

- <u>Tess's</u> favorite movies are comedies.

When the possessive has two syllables and ends in an *s* or *z* sound, just add an apostrophe.

- <u>Spyros'</u> parents are from Greece.

In Plural Possessives

Use an apostrophe to form the possessive of a plural noun ending in *s*.

- The <u>boys'</u> bathroom is off limits.

Plural nouns not ending in *s* require an apostrophe and *s*.

- The <u>women's</u> bathroom is open.

In Shared Possessives

When more than one noun shares possession, add an apostrophe and *s* to the last noun.

- <u>Rosa and Carla's</u> project fell into a mud puddle.

hey'll

Parts of Speech

Our language is like a spider's web. Spiders know exactly how to weave long-lasting and beautiful webs. To ensure a web's strength, spiders carefully link many different threads. In language, we link different types of words to create strong sentences. Just as webs blow away without their connecting threads, language falls apart without the correct parts of speech. By studying the parts of speech, you can learn how to weave words into strong and beautiful sentences.

Nouns

A noun names a person, place, thing, or idea.

Persons Nathan, mother, plumber

Places Idaho, grocery store, front yard

Things ball, candy, toolbox

Ideas anger, shyness, nervousness

Common and Proper Nouns

A common noun names a general person, place, thing, or idea. Common nouns begin with lowercase letters.

- man, dog, singer, river, country

A proper noun names a specific person, place, thing, or idea. It is always capitalized.

- Babe Ruth, Black Labrador, Nile River, Ireland

Concrete and Abstract Nouns

A concrete noun names something that may be touched or seen.

- book, bed, car

An abstract noun names something that cannot be touched or seen.

- love, pain, joy, imagination

Singular and Plural Nouns

A singular noun names only one person, place, thing, or idea.

- friend, lake, pencil, fear

A plural noun names more than one person, place, thing, or idea.

- friends, lakes, pencils, fears

Sheila (proper noun)

loves (verb)

juicy (adjectiv

Uses of Nouns

Nouns may be used as subjects, predicates, or possessives.

A subject noun either does something or is the thing being referred to.

- Sophia made dinner for Elena. (*Sophia* is the subject because she did something: *made dinner.*)

- Dinner was prepared on time. (*Dinner* is the subject because it is the thing being referred to.)

A predicate noun renames the subject. It connects to the subject with a linking verb.

- Dinner was lasagna. (The noun *lasagna* renames the subject *dinner.* It is linked by the verb *was.*)

A possessive noun shows possession or ownership.

- Sophia made the lasagna using Cynthia's recipe. (The *'s* added to *Cynthia* shows that the recipe belongs to her.)

Nouns as Objects

Nouns may be direct objects, indirect objects, or the objects of a preposition.

A noun is a direct object when it receives the action of the verb.

- Sophia made Elena dinner. (*Dinner* is the direct object because it is the thing being made.)

A noun is an indirect object when it names the person to or for whom something is being done.

- Sophia made Elena dinner. (*Elena* is the indirect object because dinner was being made for her.)

A noun is an object of a preposition when it is part of a prepositional phrase.

- Sophia made dinner using the ingredients from Cynthia's recipe. (The noun *recipe* is the object. The preposition is *from.* The prepositional phrase is *from Cynthia's recipe.*)

apples. (noun)

21

Pronouns

A **pronoun** replaces a noun. The most common pronouns are called personal pronouns.

- Juan fell off the ladder.
- <u>He</u> fell off the ladder.

Uses of Personal Pronouns

Personal pronouns include subject pronouns, object pronouns, and possessive pronouns.

A **subject pronoun** is the subject of a sentence.

Singular <u>He</u> painted beautiful pictures.

Plural <u>They</u> hang in a museum.

Singular I, you, he, she, it

Plural we, you, they

An **object pronoun** is used after an action verb or in a prepositional phrase.

- I painted <u>these</u>. (*These* comes after the action verb *painted*.)
- You can hang your picture below <u>them</u>. (*Them* is the object in the prepositional phrase *below them*.)

A **possessive pronoun** shows possession or ownership.

- Owen ate all of <u>his</u> lunch. (*His* comes before the noun *lunch*.)
- The food was <u>mine</u>. (*Mine* may stand alone.)

Pronouns that come before a noun my, your, his, her, its, our, their

Pronouns that stand alone mine, yours, his, hers, ours, theirs

Tip

The form of the pronouns in your sentences must agree with the words they replace.

- <u>Eva</u> had a lot of free time after <u>she</u> gave up piano lessons. (The pronoun *she* and the word it replaces, *Eva*, agree because they are both singular.)
- Eva's <u>sisters</u> were still very busy because <u>they</u> continued to take piano lessons. (The pronoun *they* and the word it replaces, *sisters*, agree because they are both plural.)

First-, Second-, and Third-Person Pronouns

These pronouns indicate whether the speaker is speaking, listening, or being spoken about.

A **first-person pronoun** replaces the name or names of a speaker.

- I enjoy watching movies. (*I* replaces the speaker's name.)
- We enjoy watching movies at the theater. (*We* replaces the names of two or more speakers.)

A **second-person pronoun** replaces the name of the person or thing being spoken to.

- Jennifer, do you want to see a movie tonight? (*You* replaces the name *Jennifer*, the person being spoken to.)
- If you boys are going, you will have to buy the tickets. (*You* replaces *boys*.)

A **third-person pronoun** replaces the name of the person or thing being discussed.

- Kevin said he would only watch an action movie. (*He* replaces *Kevin*, the person being discussed.)
- The boys said they would like to leave early to buy the tickets. (*They* replaces *boys*, who are the people being discussed.)

Verbs

A **verb** shows action or connects the subject to another word in the sentence. Verbs can be action, linking, or helping verbs.

Verbs take on many different forms. They can be singular or plural, active or passive, regular or irregular.

In addition to the present, past, and future tenses of verbs, there are special tenses of verbs called present perfect, past perfect, and future perfect.

Action Verbs

An **action verb** shows what the subject is doing. It makes the writing more clear.

- Lina jogs a lot.
- She watches cross-country races on TV.

Linking Verbs

A linking verb links a subject to a noun or an adjective in the predicate part of the sentence.

- Jane is an athlete. (The verb *is* connects the subject *Jane* to the noun *athlete*.)
- She feels tired after a long run. (The verb *feels* links the subject *she* to the adjective *tired*.)

Verbs for states of being is, are, was, were, am, been

Other linking verbs feel, look, seem, smell, taste, turn, etc.

Helping Verbs

A helping verb comes before the main verb in a sentence. It helps show action and time.

- Lina had to go to the dentist. (The verb *had* shows that the action *go to the dentist* occurred in the past.)
- Lina will get braces soon. (The verb *will* shows a future action that will take place.)

Helping verbs am, is, are, was, were, will, shall, been, could, would, should, must, can, may, might, have, had, has, do, did

Singular and Plural Verbs

Use a singular verb when the subject of a sentence is singular.

- Harry loves banana nut bread. (The subject *Harry* and the verb *loves* are both singular.)

Use a plural verb when the subject of the sentence is plural.

- Nuts make the bread more filling. (The subject *nuts* and the verb *make* are both plural.)

Active and Passive Voice

A verb is in the active voice when the subject is doing the action.

- Rory sang the "National Anthem." (The verb, *sang*, is active because the subject, *Rory*, is doing the action.)

A verb is passive when the subject does not do the action.

- The "National Anthem" was sung by Rory. (The verb, *was sung*, is passive because the subject, the *"National Anthem,"* is not doing the action.)

Regular Verbs

Most verbs are regular. By adding -ed to the end of a regular verb, you show that the action happened in the past. By using a helping verb, you state a past, present, or future action.

Past	Present	Future
I baked.	I bake.	I will bake.
I have baked.		

Irregular Verbs

Some verbs are irregular. An irregular verb does not end in -ed when you state a past action or when you use a helping verb with it.

Past	Present	Future
I ran. I have run.	I run.	I will run.

Some irregular verbs are listed below. The tense used with the helping verbs *has*, *have*, *had* is called the *past participle*.

Present Tense	Past Tense	Past Participle
am, be	was, were	been
begin	began	begun
bite	bit	bitten
blow	blew	blown
break	broke	broken
bring	brought	brought
catch	caught	caught
come	came	come
cost	cost	cost
cut	cut	cut
dive	dove, dived	dived
do	did	done
draw	drew	drawn
drink	drank	drunk
drive	drove	driven
eat	ate	eaten
fall	fell	fallen
fight	fought	fought
fly	flew	flown
get	got	gotten
give	gave	given
go	went	gone
grow	grew	grown
hang	hung	hung
hide	hid	hidden, hid
hit	hit	hit
hurt	hurt	hurt
know	knew	known
lay	laid	laid
lead	led	led
let	let	let
lie	lay	lain
lose	lost	lost
make	made	made
put	put	put
ride	rode	ridden
ring	rang	rung
run	ran	run
say	said	said
see	saw	seen
set	set	set
shake	shook	shaken
shine	shone	shone
shrink	shrank	shrunk
shut	shut	shut
sing	sang	sung
sit	sat	sat
speak	spoke	spoken
spring	sprang	sprung
steal	stole	stolen
swim	swam	swum
swing	swung	swung
take	took	taken
teach	taught	taught
tear	tore	torn
throw	threw	thrown
wear	wore	worn

Verb Tense

The time in which the verb shows action is called **tense**. Tense is shown by endings (*walk<u>ed</u>*) and by helping verbs (*<u>will</u> walk*), or by both (*<u>will have</u> walk<u>ed</u>*).

The **present tense** shows an action that is happening now or that happens often.

- Akemi <u>likes</u> the flute.
- She <u>plays</u> often.

The **past tense** shows an action that happened at a certain time in the past.

- Akemi <u>liked</u> the flute.
- She <u>played</u> often.

The **future tense** shows an action that will happen later. Use such helping verbs as *will* or *shall* before the main verb.

- Akemi <u>will like</u> the concert again next year.
- She <u>shall play</u> the flute often.

The **present perfect tense** shows an action that is still happening. Use *has* or *have* before the main verb to form the present perfect tense.

- Tim <u>has juggled</u> the oranges for an hour.

The **past perfect tense** shows an action that began and was finished in the past. Use *had* before the main verb to form the past perfect tense.

- Jessica <u>had juggled</u> the oranges for 10 minutes.

The **future perfect tense** shows an action that will begin in the future and end at a certain time in the future. Use *will have* or *shall have* to form the future perfect tense.

- Anna <u>will have juggled</u> the oranges for two hours.

Adjectives

An **adjective** is a word that describes a noun or pronoun. The different forms of adjectives are positive, comparative, and superlative.

Tip

Articles like *a*, *the*, and *an* are adjectives.

Positive Adjectives

A **positive adjective** describes a noun without comparing it to anything or anyone.

- An elephant is <u>big</u>.

Special positive adjectives good, bad, many

Comparative Adjectives

A **comparative adjective** compares two people, places, things, or ideas.

- An elephant is <u>bigger</u> than a lion. (The ending *-er* is added to one-syllable adjectives.)
- An elephant is <u>more forgetful</u> than a mouse. (You usually add *more* before an adjective with two or more syllables.)

Special comparative adjectives better, worse, more, less

Superlative Adjectives

A **superlative adjective** compares three or more people, places, things, or ideas.

- An elephant is the <u>biggest</u> animal I've seen at the zoo. (Add the ending *-est* to one-syllable adjectives.)
- A lion is the <u>most frightening</u> animal I've seen at the zoo. (You usually add *most* before an adjective with two or more syllables.)

Special superlative adjectives best, worst, most, least

Adverbs

An **adverb** describes a verb, adjective, or another adverb. Most adverbs show where, when, or how. As with adjectives, adverbs can be positive, comparative, or superlative.

Positive Adverbs

A **positive adverb** does not make a comparison.

- Miguel works <u>hard</u> all day long.

Special positive adverbs well, badly, poorly

Comparative Adverbs

A **comparative adverb** is formed by adding *-er* to one-syllable adverbs, or by adding the word *more* or *less* before longer adverbs.

- Miguel works <u>harder</u> than other kids his age.
- Miguel works <u>more often</u> than many of his friends.

Special comparative adverbs better, worse, less

Superlative Adverbs

A **superlative adverb** is formed by adding -*est* to one-syllable adverbs, or by using the word *most* or *least* before longer adverbs.

- Miguel works <u>hardest</u> in the morning.
- Miguel works <u>most often</u> at his desk.

Special superlative adverbs
best, worst, least

Tip

Be sure to use *good* and *well* correctly. *Good* is an adjective and *well* is most often an adverb. For example:
I had a <u>good</u> day because I felt <u>well</u>.

Prepositions

A **preposition** shows the relation of a noun or pronoun to another word in the sentence.

- The puppy playfully pushed the clock <u>off</u> the table.
- The rabbit was startled and jumped <u>in</u> its cage.

Object of the Preposition

The noun or pronoun that comes after the preposition is the **object of the preposition**.

- The cat hid <u>under</u> the <u>table</u>. (*Table* is the object of the preposition *under*.)

Prepositional Phrases

A **prepositional phrase** contains a preposition, the object of the preposition, and all descriptive words in between.

- The boa constrictor slithered <u>around the leg of the chair</u>.

Common Prepositions

about	into
above	like
across	near
after	next to
against	of
along	off
among	on
around	on top of
at	onto
before	out of
behind	outside
below	over
beneath	past
beside	since
between	through
by	to
down	toward
during	under
except	underneath
for	until
from	up
in	upon
in front of	with
inside	within
instead of	without

Interjections

An **interjection** expresses strong emotion or surprise. Use a comma or exclamation point to separate an interjection from the rest of a sentence.

- <u>Hey</u>, stop whining!
- <u>Ouch</u>! I stubbed my toe!

Conjunctions

A **conjunction** joins individual words or groups of words. The three types of conjunctions are coordinate, correlative, or subordinate.

Coordinate Conjunctions

A **coordinate conjunction** connects equal parts: two or more words, phrases, or clauses.

- The snake slithered around the tree branch <u>and</u> down the trunk. (The conjunction *and* joins two prepositional phrases.)

Coordinate conjunctions and, but, or, nor, for, so, yet

Correlative Conjunctions

Use a **correlative conjunction** in pairs.

- <u>Either</u> come <u>or</u> go, but make a decision. (*Either* and *or* work as a pair in this sentence.)

Correlative conjunctions either/or, neither/nor, both/and, not only/but, not only/also, whether/or

Subordinate Conjunctions

Use a **subordinate conjunction** to join two clauses to make a complex sentence.

- I had to finish my math homework <u>before I was allowed to go outside and play.</u>
- I'm good with numbers, <u>so I finished my homework without a problem</u>.

Subordinate conjunctions after, although, as if, because, before, if, in order that, since, so, that, though, unless, until, when, where, while

Writing Numbers

There are several rules for writing numbers. Here are some tips to follow:

Usually, numbers from one to nine are written as words. Numbers greater than 10 are usually written as numerals.

- two, five, 12, 699, 10,000

When you compare numbers, use all numerals or all words.

- The toys are popular among kids, ages 7 to 13.

Use a combination of words and numerals for very large numbers.

- 6 trillion, 30 million

Use words to begin a sentence.

- Twenty students tried out for the play, but only six got parts.

Use numerals for numbers in the following forms:

- money $4.50
- decimals 10.5
- percentages 5%
- chapters . . . . Chapter 1
- pages . . . . page 33
- addresses . . . . 6235 W. Locust
- dates . . . . October 12
- times . . . . 2:00 P.M.
- statistics . . . . . a ratio of 3 to 1

Words That Add Spark to Your Writing

It's important that your writing be interesting to you and your readers. One way to add spark to your writing is to use different types of words. Antonyms, synonyms, and homonyms will not only make your writing come alive but also give you a better understanding of the words you use.

Antonyms

An antonym is a word with an opposite meaning. Antonyms create contrast and conflict in writing. The opening of Charles Dickens' *A Tale of Two Cities* is famous for its many antonyms. The words set the stage for the conflict to come.

- "It was the <u>best</u> of times, it was the <u>worst</u> of times, it was the age of <u>wisdom</u>, it was the age of <u>foolishness</u> . . ."

Synonyms

A synonym is a word with a similar meaning. Synonyms enliven your writing and give the reader more than one way to think about your description.

- I was <u>thrilled</u> to learn the joyous news that our neighbor had just adopted a baby and would <u>happily</u> have a party to celebrate.

Homonyms

Homonyms are two words that sound the same but have different meanings.

Homophones are words that sound alike but have different spellings and different meanings.

- The <u>witch</u> liked to <u>sail</u> through the air on her broom, <u>which</u> she had bought at a garage <u>sale</u> for a good price.

Homographs are words that have the same spellings but have different origins and meanings.

- My brother needs to learn to play <u>fair</u>.
- I have tickets for the <u>fair</u> this weekend.

The Traits of Good Writing

Knowing the traits of good writing and how to use them can help your writing.

Ideas

Sending Out a Message

When you write, you're trying to get a message across to your reader. To do this, your ideas need to be presented clearly. They should be fresh, exciting, and hold the reader's attention. Support your ideas with accurate information and details, leaving your reader with new insight into the topic.

Organization

Where Should I Put Things?

When you write, you don't want the reader to get lost. How you structure your writing helps guide your reader through your story. Begin with a strong lead, or a sentence that grabs the reader's attention. Then use transitions, or phrases, to connect one idea to the next, until you lead the reader to the conclusion.

Voice

How Do I Sound?

Voice is how your writing sounds. When you find your voice, you become part of your writing. The reader, your audience, can "hear" how you feel about your subject. Write as if you are talking to a friend. Your voice should fit your topic. For example, you wouldn't write cheerfully about people crying as they wave goodbye to their friends. You would write cheerfully, however, if you were describing people celebrating a holiday.

Word Choice

Painting with Words

Words are like the colors painters use to create a picture. Your words should be colorful, rich, and lively. The right words paint the perfect picture in your reader's mind. This picture helps the reader clearly understand your message.

Sentence Fluency

Writing with Rhythm

If you had to listen to the same sound over and over again, say squeaky car brakes or a dripping faucet, you would get tired of hearing it. The same is true about sentences. Using short and long sentences creates a rhythm. And, sentences shouldn't all start the same way. When read aloud, your writing should sound pleasing to the ear.

Conventions

Catching Errors

Make your writing error-free by following the rules of language: correct spelling, capitalization, punctuation, and grammar. Place those periods properly and capitalize those proper nouns so your readers can enjoy your writing.

Presentation

Pleasing to the Eye

Think of presentation as an invitation to read a piece of writing. It's important how your writing looks to the reader. Sloppy handwriting or too many pictures can distract the reader. You want the reader to pay attention to your writing and to easily understand your message. That's why you should either neatly hand write or type your final text. Titles, illustrations, page numbers, charts, and bullets also help the reader understand information.

Sentences

A sentence begins with a capital letter, includes one or more words, and ends with a period, question mark, or exclamation point. It may ask a question, make a statement, give a command, or show strong emotion, but a sentence must always express a complete thought. The main parts of a sentence are the subject, predicate, modifier, and clause. There are different kinds of sentences: simple, compound, and complex, as well as declarative, interrogative, imperative, and exclamatory. Read on to become familiar with these kinds of sentences. Then learn how to avoid making mistakes with the words *which*, *that*, and *what*.

subject

clause

modifier

predicate

Subjects

A simple subject is the noun in a sentence that performs an action.

- My neighbor <u>Kyle</u> mowed the lawn. (*Kyle* is the simple subject.)

A complete subject is the simple subject and all of the words that describe it.

- <u>My neighbor Kyle</u> mowed the lawn. (*My neighbor Kyle* is the complete subject.)

A compound subject is made up of two or more simple subjects.

- <u>Kyle</u> and his <u>dad</u> enjoyed a big breakfast together.

Predicates

A simple predicate is the verb that tells something about the subject.

- Kyle <u>mowed</u> the lawn early in the morning. (*Mowed* tells what the subject did.)

A complete predicate is the simple predicate and all of the words that describe it.

- Kyle <u>mowed the lawn early in the morning</u>. (The complete predicate is *mowed the lawn early in the morning*.)

A compound predicate is made up of two or more simple predicates.

- Kyle <u>set</u> the table and <u>poured</u> the juice.

Modifiers

A **modifier** is a word or group of words that add detail to the sentence. A modifier can be an adjective or an adverb.

- Kyle mowed the lawn <u>quickly</u> and <u>evenly</u>. (*Quickly* and *evenly* are adverbs that describe in detail how Kyle mowed the lawn.)

Types of Sentences

A **simple sentence** expresses one complete thought. It has only one independent clause, but it may have a compound subject or a compound predicate and one or two phrases.

- My back hurts. (simple sentence)
- They <u>feel</u> tight and <u>will be</u> sore for a while. (This simple sentence includes a compound predicate, *feel* and *will be*.)
- My <u>shoulders</u> and <u>back muscles</u> <u>feel</u> tight and <u>are</u> sore. (This simple sentence includes both a compound subject, *shoulders* and *back muscles*, and a compound predicate, *feel* and *are*.)

A **compound sentence** is made up of two or more simple sentences that are linked by a comma and a connecting word, or conjunction, such as *and*, *but*, *so*, or by a semicolon.

- I have read about Africa, <u>but</u> I have never been there.
- I am interested in foreign countries; I hope to travel when I'm older.

A **complex sentence** has one independent clause and one or more dependent clauses.

- <u>Although Africa is thousands of miles away</u>, I'm willing to make the long trip. (*Although Africa is thousands of miles away* is a dependent clause. *I'm willing to make the long trip* stands alone as a sentence.)

A **declarative sentence** makes a statement.

- Japan is an island country.

An **interrogative sentence** asks a question.

- Did you know that Tokyo is the capital of Japan?

An **imperative sentence** gives a command.

- Take a passport if you visit Japan.

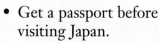

Tip

Imperative sentences don't always include the word *you*. In many cases, *you* is already understood as the subject.

- Get a passport before visiting Japan.

An **exclamatory sentence** shows emotion or surprise.

- I'm so excited about traveling to Asia!

Clauses

A **clause** is a group of related words that includes a subject and a predicate.

An **independent clause** shows a complete thought and may stand alone as a sentence.

- They wear helmets.

A **dependent clause** does not show a complete thought and may not stand alone as a sentence.

- when <u>they</u> ride their bikes

Tip

When you join a dependent clause with an independent clause, you form a complete sentence. For example, *They wear helmets when they ride their bikes.*

Phrases

A **phrase** is a group of related words that has neither a subject nor a predicate. Phrases are not sentences. They do not form a complete thought.

- The fourth-grade class (noun phrase)
- acted in a play (verb phrase)
- about the signing of the Declaration of Independence (prepositional phrase)

Tip

The combination of these three kinds of phrases creates a complete sentence: *The fourth-grade class acted in a play about the signing of the Declaration of Independence.*

Which vs. That

Writers are often unsure when to use the words which and that. Both words add information and detail to sentences. The trick is to figure out if the information is essential to the sentence. Follow these rules to help you use the words correctly.

Use *which* to introduce a nonessential clause—information that is not essential to the sentence. Remember to use a comma to separate the added information from the main part of the sentence.

- Our neighbor's house, <u>which</u> looks like a gingerbread house, is 75 years old.

Use *that* to introduce an essential clause—information that is essential to the sentence. No comma is necessary when using the word *that*.

- The house <u>that</u> looks like a gingerbread house was built 75 years ago.

Which vs. What

Which is used when something can be counted, and *what* is used when something cannot be counted.

- Francesca couldn't decide <u>which</u> skirt to buy. (In this case, Francesca must choose among more than one skirt.)
- Francesca often has difficulty deciding <u>what</u> to buy. (In this case, it's impossible to determine how many things Francesca has difficulty deciding to buy.)

Paragraphs

Think of a paragraph as a human body, in which the brain is in control. In a paragraph, the topic sentence is like the brain. It sets the direction of the entire paragraph. The rest of the sentences are like the parts of the body. They follow the direction of the topic sentence by adding the details and examples that make the paragraph work.

A **paragraph** consists of the topic sentence, the body, and the closing sentence.

Topic Sentence

The **topic sentence** is usually the first sentence in a paragraph. It tells the reader what the paragraph will be about. A topic sentence includes a specific topic and focus.

The **topic** must be simple enough for a brief paragraph. A paragraph on the history of the United States, for example, would be too large a topic. A paragraph on the history of the Washington Monument, however, would work.

Too large Rivers

Just right The Mississippi River

Topic sentence

Body

The **focus** is the specific information you want to provide about the topic. For example, a paragraph on the history of the Washington Monument might focus on the materials used to build the monument.

Topic a paragraph on Labrador Retrievers

Focus a paragraph on Labradors hunting ducks

Topic a paragraph on the Mississippi River

Focus a paragraph on how river barges on the Mississippi are used to transport goods to Illinois

Body

The **body** is the middle part of a paragraph. It is made up of the sentences between the topic sentence and the closing sentence. These sentences give the reader additional information about the topic.

Closing Sentence

The **closing sentence** ends the paragraph. It sums up the information in the paragraph and explains what it all means.

Read the following paragraph about eating spaghetti, and see how it is divided into a clear beginning, middle, and end.

Eating spaghetti is fun but a little dangerous. The dangerous part is when the food on your fork falls off. This happens to me all the time—then, plop! The meatball falls into my lap and the spaghetti goes on my shirt and makes a big red spot from the sauce. But the fun part of eating spaghetti is the sound and taste. The slurping sound is a little rude, but it reminds me how much I love spaghetti. The long, thin noodles taste good, and my grandma's special red sauce makes them even better. For me, spaghetti is the perfect meal, even if it is messy.

Closing sentence

Types of Paragraphs

The four most common types of paragraphs are descriptive, narrative, persuasive, and expository.

Descriptive Paragraphs

A **descriptive paragraph** describes a person, place, thing, or idea. Use words that help the reader see, hear, smell, taste, and feel what you are writing about. It's important to describe color, size, and sound. The reader should feel as though he or she is with you.

Sample Descriptive Paragraph

The kitchen is the best room in my house. It's always warm and inviting. My family and friends gather there to eat and talk about the day. I especially love the kitchen around dinnertime, when the smells of spices and cooking food float through the air. The clanging sounds of plates and silverware remind me that I'll soon fill my stomach with delicious, homemade food.

Narrative Paragraphs

A **narrative paragraph** tells a story about a particular experience. The reader should feel drawn into your story and interested in what you'll tell about next. Be sure to use descriptive words and details to make the experience seem more real.

Sample Narrative Paragraph

I woke up early on Saturday morning to the sound of my alarm clock buzzing in my ear. I had no time to waste, hopped out of bed, threw on some clothes, and laced up my soccer shoes. I dashed outside in time to see the sun rise. I began to practice right away. An hour had passed before I felt good about my dribbling and control of the ball. Another hour went by before I felt satisfied with my left kick. By noon, I was drenched in sweat, sunburned, and sore all over. I was ready for tomorrow's game the next day.

What is the focus of this narrative paragraph? Read to find out.

Persuasive Paragraphs

A **persuasive paragraph** tells the writer's opinion about a topic. It also tries to convince the reader of the writer's point of view. In a persuasive paragraph, give facts and examples to help prove that your opinion is correct. The more examples you give, the more likely you are to persuade the reader.

Sample Persuasive Paragraph

Two annual holidays in this country are Mother's Day and Father's Day. Twice a year kids have a chance to let their parents know how much they mean to them. So it's only fair that kids get a special holiday, too. Kids need to know how much their parents care about them. There should be cards that say, "Happy Kid's Day!" Kids should get the day off from school to celebrate their special day, and parents should do whatever their kids want them to on that day. Kid's Day would definitely be the most popular holiday of the year!

Expository Paragraphs

An **expository paragraph** gives information about a topic. It explains things, gives directions, or tells how to do something. It's important to use transition words in an expository paragraph, such as first, second, finally, and however. These words make the paragraph flow more smoothly and help the reader understand the explanation.

Sample Expository Paragraph

The secret to making good pizza is using only the best ingredients. First make your own pizza dough. That's easy once you learn how to knead the dough and stretch it out. Next get the cheeses and toppings you want to put on. Grate one, two or even three kinds of cheese. I like mushrooms, onions, and green peppers on my pizza. Chop the toppings into small pieces. Now, pour the sauce over the pizza dough, sprinkle the cheeses on top, and then add the toppings. At last you are ready to bake. Your delicious pizza is only 20 minutes away.

Basic Rules of Spelling

Learning to spell is like learning to play a new game. Once you learn the basic rules, you'll always remember them. Keep in mind that there are always exceptions to the rules, so it's a good idea to check a dictionary if you're unsure. Here are some tips to help you become a better speller:

i Before e

For words spelled with an *i* and *e* together, remember the phrase, "*i* before *e*, except after *c*."

- receive, believe

The last part of that rule is: "except for words that sound like *weigh* and *neigh*."

- sleigh, neighbor

Silent e

If a word ends with a silent *e*, drop the *e* before adding a suffix (ending) that begins with a vowel.

- use   using   usable
- believe believing believable
- shake   shaking   shakable

Tip

Do not drop the e when the suffix begins with a consonant (-*ful*, -*ness*). For example: hopeful, shameful, sameness, bareness

Consonant Ending

If a one-syllable word with a short vowel needs an ending like -*ed* or -*ing*, double the final consonant.

- mat   matted
- set   setting

Words Ending in y

For plurals of words that end in *y*, change the *y* to an *i* and add -*es*. If the word ends in *ey*, add an *s*.

- country   countries
- monkey   monkeys

Would you like a piece of pie?

Neigh!

More Spelling Tips

Make a Dictionary

It may be helpful to keep a notebook of the words you have trouble spelling. When you see an unfamiliar word, look closely at the word, say it, and write it in your notebook. You can create your own dictionary by alphabetizing the words you've written down. By writing the words and organizing them alphabetically, you'll have an easier time remembering how to spell them in the future.

Read from Bottom to Top

After you write, reread your work from bottom to top. This will help you focus on each word you have written and allow you to catch errors.

Tip

Another helpful strategy is to hold an index card under each line. This will help you focus on each line without being distracted by the other lines on the page.

Mark Unfamiliar Words

Circle or underline the words that are difficult for you. After you write, return to the words you have marked and look them up in a dictionary—maybe the one you created!

Tip

Ask a friend, family member, or teacher to read your writing. Someone who hasn't read your work yet may catch mistakes you haven't noticed.

Basic Rules of Writing

Writing is your chance to let your imagination run free and express your feelings. It is a fun and rewarding process that allows you to think deeply about many topics. As a writer, you can always change your style, use different words, and experiment with new topics. You never stop learning how to write. Here are a few basic rules to help you develop your writing:

Write What You Know

Write about the things that interest you. You're more likely to write well if you not only understand but also feel strongly about your topic. Your reader will know you've written from the heart.

> What kinds of things do you know a lot about? Try writing about one of these ideas.

Do Your Research

For some types of writing, it's a good idea to do research before you begin writing. Facts and details will make your words more believable. Before you go to the library, write down everything you already know about your topic. You'll see how much more information you need to make your report strong. You might even talk to someone about your topic.

Stick to the Topic

It's important to think about ways to keep your writing centered on your topic. Decide what readers need to know. If you're writing about a pet, focus on what it looks like and give details about how it acts and why you like it.

Drafts

Now write a first draft. Write as though you are telling a story to your friends, giving all the details but not worrying about how you sound. It's all right to have mistakes in a first draft. It's a good idea to write in the margins, cross out words, draw arrows, and move words around. A draft does not need to look neat. The important thing is to put your thoughts on paper. You can organize them better in later drafts.

Editing Do's

- combine short sentences
- vary your sentence beginnings
- correct sentence errors
- use active verbs
- use specific nouns
- use descriptive modifiers

Combine Short, Choppy Sentences

When you use a lot of short sentences, your writing may sound choppy and rough. Try to combine a few short sentences to balance your writing and ease the flow of words. Read the examples below and see how smoothly the sentences flow when some of them are combined.

- Lisa walked home from school. She walked with her friend Angela. Lisa and Angela were great friends. They liked to play together. They never argued.

Now read the sentences when some of them are combined.

- Lisa and her friend Angela walked home from school. They were great friends. They liked to play together and never argued.

Tip

When writing a draft, leave a blank line in between each written line. That gives you room to cross out words, draw arrows, and move words around.

Reread and Edit

You don't need to be a perfect speller or to have mastered the rules of grammar to be a good writer. It is important, however, that you correct as many errors as possible before finishing a piece of writing. This may mean that you reread your work over and over until you're sure you've caught all your mistakes. In doing this, it's a good idea to make a checklist of things to look for. Then ask a friend or teacher to check your work for errors.

Vary Your Sentence Beginnings

Make sure your sentences begin in different ways. If you start each sentence or paragraph in the same way, your writing may seem dull and boring.

- Willie yawned loudly and stretched his arms. Willie slowly got out of bed. Willie walked down the hall to the bathroom. Willie splashed water on his face, brushed his teeth, and felt ready to start the day.

Begin with the same first sentence.

- Willie yawned loudly and stretched his arms.

Use a pronoun and combine the two short sentences:

- He slowly got out of bed and walked down the hall to the bathroom.

Begin the last sentence with a clause.

- After splashing water on his face and brushing his teeth, Willie felt ready to start the day.

Correct Sentence Errors

Sentence fragments, run-on sentences, and rambling sentences are three of the most common errors people make in writing. They make your writing choppy and hard to read. Learn how to avoid these common errors.

A **sentence fragment** does not express a complete thought.

- Doesn't know right from wrong. (The subject is missing.)

Fix the fragment by adding a subject.

- Peter doesn't know right from wrong.

A **run-on sentence** occurs when two or more sentences are joined without punctuation or the correct linking word.

- Peter doesn't know right from wrong he is always getting into trouble.

Fix the run-on sentence by making two separate sentences.

- Peter doesn't know right from wrong. He is always getting into trouble.

A **rambling sentence** occurs when too many short sentences are joined with the word *and*.

- Peter doesn't know right from wrong and he is always getting into trouble and he misses school a lot too and he also refuses to do his homework and he likes to act tougher than everyone else.

Fix the rambling sentence by getting rid of some of the *and*'s and making separate sentences.

- Peter doesn't know right from wrong. He is always getting into trouble, and he misses school a lot. He also refuses to do his homework. He likes to act tougher than everyone else.

Use Active Verbs

Verbs are the force behind sentences. As action words, they drive your writing. Strong action verbs can make your writing come alive for the reader.

- The ice skater <u>glided</u> across the ice like a swan. She <u>twirled</u> gracefully and <u>leaped</u> high in the air. The audience <u>erupted</u> in applause when she finished.

Use Specific Nouns

General nouns like *fruit*, *flowers*, and *dogs* do not always give a complete picture. Use words like *strawberry*, *roses*, and *Golden Retriever* to be more specific and paint a colorful picture for your reader.

Use Descriptive Adjectives and Adverbs

The right adjectives and adverbs can add spark to your writing and draw readers into your work. Read the examples below and see how the use of adjectives and adverbs add color to otherwise dull sentences.

Poor use of adjectives and adverbs:

- The rain fell <u>hard</u> while the wind blew <u>loudly</u>.

Better use of adjectives and adverbs:

- The <u>harsh</u> rain fell on the <u>soggy</u> ground while the wind blew <u>fiercely</u>.

> **Tip**
>
> Don't overuse modifiers. Too many adjectives and adverbs can make your writing sound forced and false.

You might want to use the checklist below to make sure you have looked for these things as you reread.

Rereading Checklist

____ Did I write about something that interests me?

____ Did I write clear and complete sentences?

____ Did I write both short and long sentences?

____ Did I begin my sentences in different ways?

Proofreading

In revising your work or that of others, it is helpful to use proofreading symbols. As you make corrections to the text, you can use standard proofreading symbols to show exactly what kinds of changes you want to make. Read on for some of the most common proofreading symbols.

Proofreading Symbols

⊙	add a period
#	add a space
cap or ≡	capitalization
l.c. or ℓ	make a lowercase letter
n.c.	not clear
∧	omission, add something
¶	paragraph
?	unclear
Sp.	spelling
tr	switch the positions of words
✔	check this out
ℰ	take something out
w.c.	word choice

¶ Yesterday Mom and I went to the store⊙ we looked for snacks for my sleepover party on Friday night. We bought pizza and ice cream for desert. My Mom even let me get sprinkles candy to put on our ice cream. I can't wait until sleepover!

Proofreading Checklist

Use this checklist to edit and proofread your final draft:

Punctuation

____ Did I end each sentence with a punctuation mark?

____ Did I use commas in a series (*My mom, Seth, and I*)?

____ Did I use commas before conjunctions (*and, or, but*)?

____ Did I punctuate dialogue correctly?

Capitalization

____ Did I begin each sentence with a capital letter?

____ Did I capitalize nouns that name specific people, places, things, and ideas?

Spelling

____ Did I check for spelling, either with a dictionary or on a computer spell-checker?

Tip

Don't forget that a dictionary and computer spell-checker are excellent tools to help you correct spelling errors.
But beware! Computer spell-checkers won't catch the use of the wrong homophone. For example:

I will <u>bee</u> home soon.
really should be
I will <u>be</u> home soon.

49

Commonly Misused Words

Below is a list of commonly misused words. These words sound the same or similar or are often confused with each other. Read through each set of words. Then read the examples. If you are ever unsure about which word to use, consult a dictionary.

accept, except
I <u>accept</u> your offer to work here.
I have everything I need <u>except</u> for the green paint.

a lot
Mike hopes to make <u>a lot</u> of money in his new job.

already, all ready
I <u>already</u> took my weekly spelling test.
I'm <u>all ready</u> to go to dinner.

bare, bear
It's too cold to walk around in <u>bare</u> feet.
A <u>bear</u> sleeps in winter.

blew, blue
The wind <u>blew</u> gently.
The sky was clear <u>blue</u>.

by, buy
The plane whizzed <u>by</u> overhead.
Alton wants to <u>buy</u> a new coat for winter.

can, may
<u>Can</u> Shane win the pie-eating contest?
<u>May</u> I go to the carnival on Saturday?

cent, scent, sent
A penny is worth one <u>cent</u>.
The flower shop had a strong <u>scent</u>.
My dad <u>sent</u> my mom flowers.

chose, choose
Antonia <u>chose</u> to walk home from school.
They often <u>choose</u> to walk home from school.

close, clothes
<u>Close</u> the door, please.
Grandpa has worn the same <u>clothes</u> since 1977.

creak, creek
Old and worn floors sometimes <u>creak</u> when you walk on them.
The water in the <u>creek</u> flows quietly.

dear, deer
My friends are <u>dear</u> to me.
<u>Deer</u> are shy animals.

desert, dessert
The <u>desert</u> is dry and hot.
Rodrigo always saves room for <u>dessert</u>.

dew, do, due
I love the feel of morning <u>dew</u> on my bare feet.
Bart forgot to <u>do</u> his chores last night.
Homework is always <u>due</u> at the beginning of class.

doesn't, don't
Huang <u>doesn't</u> like boxing.
I <u>don't</u>, either.

eye, I
I can wink one <u>eye</u>.
<u>I</u> have perfect vision.

fewer, less
Hank has <u>fewer</u> baseball cards than Joseph.
Hank has <u>less</u> time to collect baseball cards.

fir, fur
<u>Fir</u> trees are evergreen trees.
Many people don't like the idea of <u>fur</u> coats.

for, four
This food is <u>for</u> you.
Jamie's little brother is <u>four</u> years old.

good, well
Have a <u>good</u> day.
Our team played <u>well</u>.

hare, hair
A <u>hare</u> looks like a big rabbit.
Dad has black <u>hair</u>.

heal, heel
That cut should <u>heal</u> soon.
Sammy injured the <u>heel</u> of his foot.

hear, here
It's hard to <u>hear</u> the TV when the buses go by outside.
Most of the time it's quiet in <u>here</u>.

hi, high
Don't forget to say <u>hi</u> to the coach for me.
The flag is flying <u>high</u>.

hole, whole
A bagel has a <u>hole</u> in the middle.
I always eat the <u>whole</u> bagel for breakfast.

hour, our
Mom takes a yoga class for an <u>hour</u> on Wednesday nights.
<u>Our</u> family believes that exercise is important.

its, it's
The cat licked <u>its</u> paws.
<u>It's</u> a very cute kitten.

knew, new	Kim <u>knew</u> all of the answers on the game show. She bought a <u>new</u> dress for the occasion.
knight, night	Fairy tales often involve a <u>knight</u> in shining armor. The stars shine brightly at <u>night</u>.
knot, not	Sailors know how to make and undo every kind of <u>knot</u>. I am <u>not</u> very good with my hands.
knows, nose	My teacher <u>knows</u> a lot about the planet Mars. Margo has freckles on her <u>nose</u>.
lay, lie	<u>Lay</u> the pillow on the bed. <u>Lie</u> down and take a nap.
lead, led	It's important to make sure there isn't any <u>lead</u> in the water. The mayor <u>led</u> the city parade.
loose, lose	My shoelaces came <u>loose</u> in gym. I thought for sure that I would <u>lose</u>.
mail, male	The <u>mail</u> is delivered six days a week. A <u>male</u> is a man.
main, Maine, mane	My <u>main</u> concern is that I'll miss my flight. The state of <u>Maine</u> is famous for its delicious blueberries. A horse has a <u>mane</u> of hair on its neck.
meat, meet	Vegetarians don't eat <u>meat</u>. My friends and I <u>meet</u> every Sunday morning for breakfast.
oar, or, ore	Use an <u>oar</u> to row the boat. We can take a speedboat <u>or</u> a sailboat. <u>Ore</u> is a mineral that contains metal.
one, won	Liza's family has <u>one</u> car. Elizabeth <u>won</u> the race for class president.
pain, pane	I was in <u>pain</u> after the book fell on my foot. The window <u>pane</u> needed to be washed.
pair, pare, pear	Ted wore his new <u>pair</u> of cowboy boots. To <u>pare</u> an apple means to peel it. I usually eat a juicy <u>pear</u> for dessert.

passed, past	Ramon had already <u>passed</u> several gas stations. It's best to think ahead and not dwell on the <u>past</u>.
peace, piece	Many politicians speak of working toward world <u>peace</u>. Joy asked for a small <u>piece</u> of pumpkin pie.
plain, plane	Jan wore a <u>plain</u> dress to her wedding. As a result of bad weather, the <u>plane</u> took off an hour late.
pore, pour, poor	A <u>pore</u> is a tiny opening in the skin. Would you <u>pour</u> the milk, please? I felt <u>poor</u> after I spent my allowance.
read, red	I <u>read</u> the book in just one sitting. Damien has bright <u>red</u> hair.
right, write	Is this the <u>right</u> place to sign up for the karate class? Did you <u>write</u> a thank-you letter to Grandpa?
road, rode, rowed	The <u>road</u> was dusty and rocky. We <u>rode</u> horses around the corral. Sumi <u>rowed</u> the boat to shore.
sea, see	Adrian has always liked the salty air by the <u>sea</u>. Alma can't <u>see</u> very well without her glasses.
seam, seem	The <u>seam</u> in Melvin's shirt was unraveling. He didn't <u>seem</u> to care, though.
sew, so, sow	My mom taught me how to <u>sew</u> when I was just ten years old. Her car had a flat tire, <u>so</u> she was late. A gardener must <u>sow</u> seeds to grow plants.
sit, set	May I <u>sit</u> down next to you? Latoya carefully <u>set</u> her tea on the glass table.
some, sum	Priya sold <u>some</u> of her old sweaters to earn extra money. The <u>sum</u> of 10 and 10 is 20.
son, sun	I'd like to have both a <u>son</u> and a daughter. The <u>sun</u> finally came out from behind the clouds.
stationery, stationary	Fiona writes letters on fancy <u>stationery</u>. My <u>stationary</u> bike doesn't go anywhere when I pedal.

tail, tale	The dog wagged its <u>tail</u> excitedly. Javier likes to tell <u>tales</u> about his family.
than, then	I'm taller <u>than</u> you. Let's go shopping and <u>then</u> go to lunch.
their, there, they're	Yvonne and her sister went to visit <u>their</u> grandparents. Juan likes to go over <u>there</u> because the kids have a lot of toys. I think <u>they're</u> nice people.
threw, through	The pitcher <u>threw</u> the ball hard and fast. The dog jumped <u>through</u> hoops at the circus.
to, too, two	Dad dislikes going <u>to</u> the dentist. I am <u>too</u> tired to cook dinner for the family tonight. Drake has <u>two</u> younger sisters.
waist, waste	Niles complains that his <u>waist</u> is getting too big. Pierre doesn't like to <u>waste</u> too much of his time.
wait, weight	Julio is impatient and refuses to <u>wait</u> for anyone. It's hard to lose <u>weight</u> if you don't exercise.
wear, where	Ruthie likes to <u>wear</u> large hoop earrings every day. Do you know <u>where</u> the Rocky Mountains are?
which, witch	<u>Which</u> dress should I wear to the concert? Zoe dressed as a <u>witch</u> for Halloween.
who's, whose	<u>Who's</u> going to take me to my swim meet? <u>Whose</u> goggles are these?
wood, would	The burning <u>wood</u> in the fireplace smelled good. <u>Would</u> you mind turning up the heat?
you're, your	<u>You're</u> going to get into trouble for skipping school. <u>Your</u> dad will be very upset.

54

Index